Fighting Irishology Trivia Challenge

Notre Dame Fighting Irish Football

Fighting Irishology Trivia Challenge – Notre Dame Fighting Irish Football; Second Edition 2008

Published by
Kick The Ball, Ltd
8595 Columbus Pike, Suite 197
Lewis Center, OH 43035
www.TriviaGameBooks.com

Designed, Formatted, and Edited by: Tom Rippey & Paul Wilson
Researched by: Al Netzer

For information on ordering this book in bulk at reduced prices, please email us at pfwilson@trivianthology.com.

International Standard Book Number: 978-1-934372-30-2

Printed & Bound in the United States of America

Tom P. Rippey III & Paul F. Wilson

Fighting Irishology Trivia Challenge

Notre Dame Fighting Irish Football

Researched by Al Netzer

Tom P. Rippey & Paul F. Wilson, Editors

Kick The Ball, Ltd
Lewis Center, Ohio

This book is dedicated to our families and friends for your unwavering love, support, and your understanding of our pursuit of our passions. Thank you for everything you do for us and for making our lives complete.

Dear Friend,

Thank you for purchasing our ***Fighting Irishology Trivia Challenge*** game book!

We hope you enjoy it as much as we enjoyed researching and putting it together. This book can be used over and over again in many different ways. One example would be to use it in a head-to-head challenge by alternating questions between Fighting Irish football fans – or by playing as teams. Another option would be to simply challenge yourself to see how many questions you could answer correctly. No matter how you choose to use this book, you'll have fun and maybe even learn a fact or two about Fighting Irish football.

We have made every attempt to verify the accuracy of the questions and answers contained in this book. However it is still possible that from time to time an error has been made by us or our researchers. In the event you find a question or answer that is questionable or inaccurate, we ask for your understanding and thank you for bringing it to our attention so that we may improve future editions of this book. Please email us at tprippey@trivianthology.com with those observations and comments.

Have fun playing ***Fighting Irishology Trivia Challenge***!

Tom & Paul

Tom Rippey & Paul Wilson
Co-Founders, Kick The Ball, Ltd

PS – You can discover more about all of our current trivia game books by visiting us online at www.TriviaGameBooks.com.

Table of Contents

FIGHTING IRISHOLOGY TRIVIA CHALLENGE

How to Play

FIGHTING IRISHOLOGY TRIVIA CHALLENGE

Book Format:

There are four quarters, each made up of fifty questions. Each quarter's questions have assigned point values. Questions are designed to get progressively more difficult as you proceed through each quarter, as well as through the book itself. Most questions are in a four-option multiple-choice format so that you will at least have a 25% chance of getting a correct answer for some of the more challenging questions.

We've even added an *Overtime* section in the event of a tie, or just in case you want to keep playing a little longer.

Game Options:

One Player -
To play on your own, simply answer each of the questions in all the quarters, and in the overtime section, if you'd like. Use the *Player / Team Score Sheet* to record your answers and the quarter *Answer Keys* to check your answers. Calculate each quarter's points and the total for the game at the bottom of the *Player / Team Score Sheet* to determine your final score.

Two or More Players –
To play with multiple players decide if you will all be competing with each other individually, or if you will form and play as teams. Each player / team will then have its own *Player / Team Score Sheet* to record its answer. You can use the quarter *Answer Keys* to check your answers and to calculate your final scores.

The *Player / Team Score Sheets* have been designed so that each team can answer all questions or you can divide the questions up in any combination you would prefer. For example, you may want to alternate questions if two players are playing or answer every third question for three players, etc. In any case, simply record your response to your questions in the corresponding quarter and question number on the *Player / Team Score Sheet*.

A winner will be determined by multiplying the total number of correct answers for each quarter by the point value per quarter, then adding together the final total for all quarters combined. Play the game again and again by alternating the questions that your team is assigned so that you will answer a different set of questions each time you play.

You Create the Game -
There are countless other ways of using ***Fighting Irishology Trivia Challenge*** questions. It's limited only to your imagination. Examples might be using them at your tailgate or other college football related party. Players / Teams who answer questions incorrectly may have to perform a required action, or winners may receive special prizes. Let us know what other games you come up with!

Have fun!

First Quarter

1-Point Questions

1) When did Notre Dame officially adopt "Fighting Irish" as its nickname?

A) 1899
B) 1909
C) 1927
D) 1954

2) What are the colors for Notre Dame?

A) Blue and Gold
B) Blue and Yellow
C) Gold and Silver
D) Gold and Green

3) The stadium seating capacity for Notre Dame is 80,795.

A) Yes
B) No

4) How many Heisman trophy winners played at Notre Dame?

A) 3
B) 4
C) 6
D) 7

5) What is the name of the Notre Dame fight song?

A) "The Victors"
B) "Down the Field"
C) "Notre Dame Victory March"
D) "We Are the Champions"

6) What trophy does Notre Dame and USC play for annually?

A) Jeweled Shillelagh
B) Old Oaken Bucket
C) Frank Leahy Memorial Bowl
D) Golden Boot

7) New York Tribune sportswriter, Grantland Rice used what phrase to describe the Notre Dame backfield of 1924?

A) Fearsome Foursome
B) Four Horsemen
C) Steel Curtain
D) Ghost Riders

8) Who had the longest coaching tenure at Notre Dame?

A) Tyrone Willingham
B) Lou Holtz
C) Ara Parseghian
D) Knute Rockne

9) How many coaches are tied with the second longest coaching tenure at Notre Dame?

A) 2
B) 3
C) 5
D) 7

10) Which Big Ten opponent has Notre Dame played the most?

A) Michigan
B) Ohio State
C) Purdue
D) Michigan State

11) Which opponent has Notre Dame played the most?

A) Navy
B) Army
C) Michigan
D) USC

12) By what name is the stadium where Notre Dame plays its home games often referred?

A) Notre Dame Cathedral
B) The House that Rockne Built
C) Lil' Ireland
D) The Big House

13) What is Notre Dame's Mascot?

A) Irish terrier dog
B) Four-Leaf Clover
C) Leprechaun
D) Irish Guard

14) What trophy does Notre Dame and Boston College play for?

A) Megaphone Trophy
B) Shillelagh Trophy
C) Heartland Trophy
D) Ireland Trophy

15) What is the name of the stadium where Notre Dame played its home games prior to 1930?

A) Alumni Field
B) Kyle Stadium
C) Memorial Stadium
D) Cartier Field

16) What year did Notre Dame play its first football game?

A) 1874
B) 1887
C) 1895
D) 1897

17) Did Notre Dame win its first game?

A) Yes
B) No

18) What is the name of the stadium where Notre Dame plays its home games?

A) Memorial Stadium
B) Notre Dame Stadium
C) Home of the Irish
D) Knute Rockne Stadium

19) Who holds the career rushing record for Notre Dame?

A) Autry Denson
B) George Gipp
C) Darius Walker
D) Allen Pinkett

20) Who was the first consensus All-American at Notre Dame?

A) Bob Crable
B) Gus Dorais
C) Eddie Anderson
D) Raghib Ismail

21) What year did Notre Dame play its 1,000th game?

A) 1983
B) 1989
C) 1996
D) 2006

22) George Gipp held the Notre Dame career rushing mark for more then 50 years.

A) True
B) False

23) Who is the coach with the most wins at Notre Dame?

A) Bob Davie
B) Lou Holtz
C) Frank Leahy
D) Knute Rockne

24) Which two coaches are second and third with the most wins at Notre Dame?

A) Lou Holtz and Ara Parseghian
B) Knute Rockne and Ara Parseghian
C) Ara Parseghian and Frank Leahy
D) Knute Rockne and Tyrone Willingham

25) Who holds the record for passing yards in a single game at Notre Dame?

A) Jarious Jackson
B) Joe Theismann
C) Brady Quinn
D) Ron Powlus

26) Who is the career leader in tackles for Notre Dame?

A) Bob Crable
B) Mike Kovaleski
C) Courtney Watson
D) Nick Buoniconti

27) What was the first year that Notre Dame defeated Michigan?

A) 1899
B) 1900
C) 1909
D) 1921

28) What are the most consecutive bowl games Notre Dame has been to?

A) 9
B) 16
C) 22
D) 34

29) Has Notre Dame Football ever been a member of a conference?

A) Yes
B) No

30) Who holds the Notre Dame record for total yards in a single bowl game?

A) Joe Montana
B) Tony Rice
C) Brady Quinn
D) Joe Theismann

31) How many Notre Dame head coaches have been consensus All-Americans as Notre Dame football players?

A) 0
B) 1
C) 4
D) 5

32) What bowl game has Notre Dame played in the most?

A) Orange
B) Cotton
C) Rose
D) Sugar

33) Who has received the most individual national awards while at Notre Dame?

A) Tim Brown
B) Ross Browner
C) Brady Quinn
D) Raghib Ismail

34) How many total coaches has Notre Dame had?

A) 17
B) 29
C) 40
D) 44

35) What other sport did Knute Rockne coach at ND?

A) Cross country
B) Lacrosse
C) Ice hockey
D) Fencing

36) Which player has won the most Notre Dame Monogram Club MVP awards?

A) Bob Crable
B) Tim Brown
C) Brady Quinn
D) Alan Pinkett

37) Have Michigan and Notre Dame ever played on a neutral field?

A) Yes
B) No

38) What award does the outstanding Notre Dame offensive lineman receive?

A) Blue and Gold Award
B) Guardian of the Year Award
C) Blocker Award
D) Moose Krause Trophy

39) How many Notre Dame players have received the Notre Dame Monogram Club MVP Award more than once?

A) 1
B) 4
C) 5
D) 9

40) What year did the Notre Dame band first perform on the football field?

A) 1887
B) 1901
C) 1907
D) 1920

41) How many AP National Championships has Notre Dame been awarded?

A) 0
B) 5
C) 8
D) 11

42) What is the first line of the "Notre Dame Victory March"?

A) Rally sons of Notre Dame
B) We will fight in every game
C) Send a volley cheer on high
D) Shake down the thunder from the sky

43) Who was the opponent in the dedication game for the opening of Notre Dame Stadium?

A) Army
B) Navy
C) Michigan
D) Indiana

44) At what university did Lou Holtz coach just before becoming the head coach at Notre Dame?

A) University of Arkansas
B) University of Iowa
C) University of Minnesota
D) University of South Carolina

45) Who holds the ND single game rushing record?

A) Julius Jones
B) Jerome Bettis
C) Darius Walker
D) Rocky Bleier

46) What year did Notre Dame have the most consensus All-Americans?

A) 1943
B) 1966
C) 1990
D) 2002

47) How many Notre Dame head coaches lasted just one season?

A) 0
B) 1
C) 5
D) 7

48) Who holds the Notre Dame record for points scored in a single game?

A) Jerome Bettis
B) Art Smith
C) Rick Mirer
D) Joe Theismann

49) Who holds the Notre Dame career-record for points scored?

A) Autry Denson
B) Bill Wolski
C) Jerome Bettis
D) Alan Pinkett

50) What year did Notre Dame first celebrate a victory over Navy?

A) 1912
B) 1927
C) 1937
D) 1943

First Quarter Fighting Irish Cool Fact

The Notre Dame Football team helmets symbolize the Golden Dome atop the University's Administration Building on the Notre Dame Campus. Every week student managers get each helmet ready for game day by sanding them smooth prior to painting. Not just any gold paint will do, the paint used on the Fighting Irish helmets actually contains real Gold Dust!

First Quarter Answer Key

1) C – 1927 (There are several stories as to how Notre Dame came to be the "Fighting Irish". The most widely accepted is that the press coined it; alumnus Francis Wallace made it popular in his New York Daily News columns in the 1920s)
2) A – Blue and Gold (original colors were Blue & Yellow and were later changed to Blue & Gold)
3) A – Yes
4) D – 7 (Angelo Bertelli 1943, John Lujack 1947, Leon Hart 1949, John Lattner 1953, Paul Hornung 1956, John Huarte 1964, & Tim Brown 1987)
5) C – "Notre Dame Victory March" (It was written in the early 1900s by two brothers, Michael and John Shea, who were Notre Dame Graduates.)
6) A – Jeweled Shillelagh (The tradition started in 1926 with medallions. The shillelagh was introduced in 1952, an oak war club from Ireland originally presented by the Notre Dame Alumni Club of Los Angeles.)
7) B – Four Horsemen (HBs Don Miller & Jim Crowley, FB Elmer Layden, & QB Harry Stuhldreher played together from 1922-24 only losing two games, one each in 1922 & 1923 - both to Nebraska.)
8) D – Knute Rockne (13 years, 1918-1930)

9) B – 3 (Frank Leahy 1941-1943, 1946-1953, Ara Parseghian 1964-1974, & Lou Holtz 1986-1996)

10) C – Purdue (78 games)

11) A – Navy (80 games since 1927)

12) B – The House that Rockne Built (The stadium was built largely due to the success of Knute Rockne's teams. He had a lot of say on different areas of construction in and around the stadium.)

13) C – Leprechaun (The Leprechaun became the official mascot in 1965, before that, Notre Dame had a series of Irish terrier dogs, known as Clashmore Mike, for its mascot.)

14) D – Ireland Trophy (Awarded to the winner since 1995, each school has won it 5 times. The trophy was created by Notre Dame's Student Government.)

15) D – Cartier Field (Built in the late 1890s and named after 1887 Notre Dame graduate Warren Cartier, who supplied the building materials, Notre Dame's practice field is still called Cartier Field)

16) B – 1887 (November 23, 1887 against Michigan)

17) B – No (Notre Dame 0, Michigan 8)

18) B – Notre Dame Stadium (Opened in 1930 with a capacity of 54,000, it was expanded in 1997 bringing its capacity to more than 80,000.)

19) A – Autry Denson (4,318 yards on 854 attempts, 5.1 yards a carry with 43 touchdowns in 1995-98)

20) B – Gus Dorias (Quarterback in 1913, he led Notre Dame to three consecutive undefeated seasons.)

21) C – 1996 (September 5, 1996: Notre Dame 14, Vanderbilt 7)

22) A – True (From 1920, his last season, until broken by Jerome Heavens in 1978.)

23) D – Knute Rockne (105 wins)

24) A – Lou Holtz (100 wins) and Ara Parseghian (95 wins)

25) B – Joe Theismann (526 yards versus USC in 1970; 33-58 with 4 interceptions & 2 touchdowns; he also had two rushing touchdowns & one fumble.)

26) A – Bob Crable (521 tackles; played from 1978-81)

27) C – 1909 (Notre Dame 11, Michigan 3; Michigan won 8 straight games prior to 1909 and then did not play Notre Dame again for 33 years.)

28) A – 9 (1988 to 1996; From 1925 to 1969 Notre Dame had a "no bowl policy". Their current streak is 3.)

29) B – No (Notre Dame has always been an Independent in football, but is a member of the Big East Conference in all other sports.)

30) B – Tony Rice (1989 Fiesta Bowl; 288 total yards, 213 yards passing, 75 yards rushing; Notre Dame 34, West Virgina 21)

31) B – 1 (Elmer Layden 1924; member of the famed Four Horsemen, He coached Notre Dame from 1934 to 1940 with a 47-13-3 record.)

32) B – Cotton (7 times; 1969, 1970, 1977, 1978, 1987, 1992, & 1993)

33) C – Brady Quinn (4 total awards in 2006; Maxwell Award, Johnny Unitas Golden Arm Award, Cingular All-America Player of the Year, and Sammy Baugh Trophy.)

34) B – 29

35) A – Cross country (It was started in 1923 with Knute Rockne as the sport's first coach.)

36) D – Alan Pinkett (3 times, 1983, 1984, & 1985; started in 1967, it is awarded by team members.)

37) A – Yes (Notre Dame 0, Michigan 23, a game played in Toledo, Ohio in 1902)

38) B – Guardian of the Year Award (It began in 2000 and is presented by Guardian Insurance Company.)

39) D – 9 (Terry Hanratty '67-'68, Greg Collins '73-'74, Bob Crable '80-'81, Allen Pinkett '83-'84-'85, Tim Brown '86-'87, Tony Rice '88-'89, Derrick Mayes '94-'95, Autry Denson '97-'98, & Brady Quinn '05-'06)

40) A – 1887 (Notre Dame's band is the oldest college band in continuous existence. The university was established in 1842 and the band in 1845. It played at the first game vs. Michigan in 1887.)

41) C – 8 ('43, '46, '47, '49, '66, '73, '77, & '88)

42) A – Rally sons of Notre Dame

43) B – Navy (Notre Dame 26, Navy 2; Notre Dame had already played SMU at home. However the stadium's official dedication game was the 2nd home game of 1930 against Navy.)

44) C – University of Minnesota (He coached the Golden Gophers for just one season.)

45) A – Julius Jones (262 yards on 24 attempts for 10.9 yards per carry vs. Pittsburgh in 2003)

46) A – 1943 (5 consensus All-Americans: QB, Angelo Bertelli; G, Pat Filley; HB, Creighton Miller; T, Jim White; and E, John Yonakor)

47) D – 7 (J. L. Morrison 1894, H. C. Hadden 1895, James McWeeney 1899, Louis Salmon 1904, Henry J. McGlew 1905, Victor M. Place 1908, and Ed Mckeever 1944)

48) B – Art Smith (37 points; 7 rushing touchdowns and 2 PATs, versus Loyola (Chi) in 1911; Notre Dame 80, Loyola (Chi) 0; TDs were 5 points in that era.)

49) D – Alan Pinkett (320 points from 1982-85; 53 rushing touchdowns, one two-point conversion)

50) B – 1927 (Notre Dame 19, Navy 6; Baltimore, MD)

Note: All answers valid as of the end of the 2007 season, unless otherwise indicated in the question itself.

1) How many Notre Dame players have received the NCAA Silver Anniversary Award?

A) 1
B) 3
C) 6
D) 8

2) What was Notre Dame QB Paul Hornung's nickname?

A) The Golden Arm
B) The Golden Bear
C) The Golden Boy
D) The Golden Child

3) How many Notre Dame Coaches are in the College Football Hall of Fame?

A) 2
B) 3
C) 5
D) 6

4) How many different decades has the Fighting Irish won at least 85 games?

A) 0
B) 1
C) 3
D) 5

5) What year was the first undefeated season for Notre Dame (minimum 8 games)?

A) 1898
B) 1903
C) 1909
D) 1912

6) How many undefeated/untied seasons has Notre Dame had (minimum 8 games)?

A) 1
B) 4
C) 7
D) 9

7) How many undefeated seasons with one tie has Notre Dame had (minimum 8 games)?

A) 1
B) 4
C) 6
D) 9

8) Where does Notre Dame rank in all-time NCAA victories?

A) 1st
B) 2nd
C) 5th
D) 10th

9) Notre Dame has never had two different running backs rush for over 1,000 yards in the same season.

A) True
B) False

10) Which conference has Notre Dame played the least number of times?

A) Western Athletic
B) Conference USA
C) Mountain West
D) Big East

11) In what foreign country did Notre Dame play Navy in 1996?

A) Canada
B) Japan
C) Ireland
D) Australia

12) What year was Notre Dame ranked #1 by the AP for the full season?

A) 1929
B) 1938
C) 1943
D) 1988

13) Notre Dame holds the AP record for most weeks at #1 all-time?

A) True
B) False

14) Who holds the Notre Dame record for most tackles in a single game?

A) Steve Heimkreiter
B) Bob Golic
C) Chinedum Ndukwe
D) Bob Crable

15) Who holds the Notre Dame record for most pass attempts per game in a season?

A) Daryle Lamonica
B) Joe Theismann
C) Rick Mirer
D) Brady Quinn

16) What are the most sacks recorded in a single season by a Notre Dame player?

A) 7.5
B) 9
C) 13.5
D) 14

17) How many Notre Dame players hold the career record for combined punt returns and kickoff returns for TDs?

A) 2
B) 3
C) 5
D) 6

18) How many yards was Brady Quinn's longest pass play in his career at Notre Dame?

A) 62
B) 72
C) 85
D) 96

19) What is the longest winning streak for Navy in the Navy-Notre Dame series?

A) 2
B) 4
C) 5
D) 6

20) Who handed Notre Dame its worst bowl game defeat?

A) Texas A&M
B) Nebraska
C) LSU
D) Oregon State

21) Who was Notre Dame's first bowl opponent?

A) Southern California
B) Alabama
C) Stanford
D) Texas

22) In what bowl was Notre Dame's first bowl appearance?

A) Liberty Bowl
B) Cotton Bowl
C) Orange Bowl
D) Rose Bowl

23) What is Notre Dame's record in Fiesta Bowl games?

A) 0-4
B) 1-3
C) 2-2
D) 3-1

24) Who holds the Notre Dame record for most rushing yards in a bowl game?

A) Jerome Bettis
B) Alan Pinkett
C) Autry Denson
D) Elmer Layden

25) How many Super Bowl rings does current Notre Dame Head Coach Charlie Weis have?

A) 0
B) 1
C) 2
D) 4

26) How many times has a Notre Dame player been named Sugar Bowl MVP?

A) 0
B) 2
C) 4
D) 5

27) How many times has a Notre Dame player been named Cotton Bowl MVP?

A) 0
B) 2
C) 5
D) 8

28) How many Irish have been awarded a bowl MVP twice?

A) 0
B) 1
C) 3
D) 6

29) How many seasons did ND play without a head coach?

A) 0
B) 1
C) 2
D) 5

30) How many total years did Notre Dame not field a team after starting football play in 1887?

A) 0
B) 1
C) 2
D) 5

31) How many players made up the first Notre Dame Football team?

A) 8
B) 11
C) 15
D) 24

32) Which Notre Dame head coach has the only losing record?

A) Hugh Devore
B) Tyrone Willingham
C) Joe Kuharich
D) Gerry Faust

33) What are the most points Notre Dame has scored in a single game?

A) 69
B) 79
C) 104
D) 142

34) Who was Notre Dame's first opponent away from home?

A) Northwestern
B) Illinois
C) Michigan
D) Chicago

35) Which team gave Notre Dame its biggest loss in the regular season?

A) Wisconsin
B) Michigan
C) Army
D) Navy

36) Who was Notre Dame's opponent in the first ever night game at Notre Dame Stadium?

A) Michigan State
B) Navy
C) USC
D) Michigan

37) Who was the first two-time consensus All-American for Notre Dame?

A) Frank Carideo
B) John Lattner
C) Bob Crable
D) John Lujack

38) How many two-time consensus All-Americans does Notre Dame have?

A) 6
B) 8
C) 10
D) 16

39) Who is the only quarterback to pass for over 3,000 yards in a season?

A) Joe Theismann
B) Brady Quinn
C) Joe Montana
D) Jarious Jackson

40) Has a Notre Dame quarterback passed for over 10,000 yards in a career?

A) Yes
B) No

41) Who holds the ND record for receiving yards in a single game?

A) Maurice Stovall
B) Jeff Samardzija
C) Jim Seymour
D) Tim Brown

42) Who holds the ND record for receiving yards in a season?

A) Jack Snow
B) Tim Brown
C) Tom Gatewood
D) Jeff Samardzija

43) Who holds the ND record for receiving yards in a career?

A) Tim Brown
B) Tom Gatewood
C) Jeff Samardzija
D) Derrick Mayes

44) How many consensus National Championships has Notre Dame won?

A) 8
B) 10
C) 11
D) 21

45) How many Irish have been runner-up in Heisman voting?

A) 0
B) 3
C) 5
D) 7

46) How many Fighting Irish have been named *AP* Male Athlete of the Year?

A) 0
B) 1
C) 2
D) 4

47) What year did Notre Dame set the NCAA record for most offensive plays per game?

A) 1946
B) 1953
C) 1970
D) 1988

48) How many Fighting Irish have been selected consensus All-Americans?

A) 43
B) 55
C) 69
D) 79

49) How many Notre Dame Coaches have won National Coach of the Year while at Notre Dame?

A) 0
B) 2
C) 4
D) 7

50) Which actor played George Gipp in the 1940s' movie "Knute Rockne All-American"?

A) James Cagney
B) Ronald Reagan
C) Pat O'Brien
D) John Wayne

Second Quarter Fighting Irish Cool Fact

It is the most recognizable college fight song ever, the "Notre Dame Victory March". The song was honored in 1969 as the "Greatest of All Fight Songs", when college football celebrated its centennial. The tune has been borrowed by countless high schools across the country and has even been adopted by an 'Australian Rules' football team. It's generally considered to be as popular as "The Star-Spangled Banner," "God Bless America," and "White Christmas", and can even be heard in the 1980 comedy – Airplane!

Second Quarter Answer Key

1) C – 6 (Jim Lynch LB 1991, Alan Page DE 1992, Joe Theismann QB 1996, Dave Casper TE 1998, Bob Thomas K 1998, Ken MacAfee TE 2002; The award is given to former student-athletes 25 years after graduating for success in their chosen careers and community service.)
2) C – The Golden Boy (1954-56; His charismatic personality earned him the nickname.)
3) D – 6 (Dan Devine inducted in 1985, Ara Parseghian inducted in 1980, Jesse Harper inducted in 1971, Frank Leahy inducted in 1970, Knute Rockne inducted in 1951, and Lou Holtz inducted in 2008.)
4) B – 1 (91 wins in the 1970s)
5) B – 1903 (8-0-1; nine shutouts)
6) D – 9 (1919, 1920, 1924, 1929, 1930, 1947, 1949, 1973, & 1988)
7) C – 6 (1903, 1909, 1941, 1946, 1948, & 1966)
8) B – 2nd (Notre Dame has 821 total victories, second only to Michigan's 860.)
9) A – True (Though in 1978 Vagas Ferguson rushed for 1,192 yards and Jerome Heavens 728 yards.)
10) A – Western Athletic (Notre Dame has played 2 games against this conference - both against Hawaii.)

11) C – Ireland (Notre Dame 54, Navy 27; Croke Park in Dublin, Ireland)

12) C – 1943 (nine weeks at #1)

13) A – True (95 total weeks; Oklahoma is next with 91 weeks and Ohio State is third with 86 weeks.)

14) B and D – Bob Golic (26 tackles in 1978, Notre Dame 14, Michigan 28) and Bob Crable (26 tackles in 1979, Notre Dame 10, Clemson 16)

15) D – Brady Quinn (37.5 pass attempts per game in 2005; 450 in 12 games)

16) C – 13.5 (Justin Tuck 2003)

17) B – 3 (Raghib Ismail 1 punt return, 5 kickoff returns; Tim Brown 3 punt returns, 3 kickoff returns; Allen Rossum 3 punt returns, 3 kickoff returns)

18) C – 85 (2003 Notre Dame 10, Purdue 23; Quinn's first collegiate start, pass to Maurice Stovall, 3rd longest TD pass in school history.)

19) A – 2 (2 times – 1933 & 1934 and again in 1960 & 1961)

20) B – Nebraska (Notre Dame 6, Nebraska 40; Orange Bowl January 1, 1973)

21) C – Stanford (1925, Notre Dame 27, Stanford 10)

22) D – Rose Bowl (The 1925 Rose Bowl is the only one Notre Dame has played in.)

23) B – 1-3 (won in 1989; lost in 1995, 2001, & 2006)

24) A – Jerome Bettis (1992 Sugar Bowl, 150 yards on 16 attempts; Notre Dame 39, Florida 28)

25) D – 4 (All 4 as an assistant coach; 1 with the New York Giants in 1990, and 3 with the New England Patriots in 2001, 2003, & 2004)

26) B – 2 (Tom Clements, QB, 1974 and Jerome Bettis, FB, 1992)

27) D – 8 (Bob Olson, LB, 1970; Clarence Ellis, CB, 1971; Vagas Ferguson, RB, 1978; Bob Golic, LB, 1978; Joe Montana, QB,1979; Rick Mirer, QB, 1993; Devon McDonald, DE, 1993; Lee Becton, RB, 1994; The Cotton Bowl selects one offensive and one defensive MVP.)

28) A – 0 (19 Notre Dame Players have been named bowl MVPs, not one more than once.)

29) D – 5 (The team captain also served as coach for the first 5 years.)

30) C – 2 (1890 & 1891)

31) B – 11 (15 students tried out. Only 11 were selected to match the number of uniforms they had.)

32) C – Joe Kuharich (His record was 17-23-0 in his 4 seasons from 1959-1962.)

33) D – 142 (1905; Notre Dame 142, American Medical 0; every Notre Dame Starter scored.)

34) A – Northwestern (1889; Notre Dame 9, Northwestern 0; Of Notre Dame's first 34 games, from 1887-1897, all but 3 of them were home games.)

35) C – Army (1944; Notre Dame 0, Army 59; played at Yankee Stadium)

36) D – Michigan (1982; Notre Dame 23, Michigan 17)

37) A – Frank Carideo (QB, 1928-30, consensus All-American in 1929 and 1930)

38) D – 16 (Frank Carideo 1929-30, Marchy Schwartz 1930-31, Bob Dove 1941-42, George Connor 1946-47, John Lujack 1946-47, Bill Fischer 1947-48, Leon Hart 1948-49, Emil Sitko 1948-49, John Lattner 1952-53, Ross Browner 1976-77, Ken MacAfee 1976-77, Bob Crable 1980-81, Michael Stonebreaker 1988, 90, Todd Lyght 1989-90, Chris Zorich 1989-90, and Aaron Taylor 1992-93)

39) B – Brady Quinn (2 times: 3,633 yards in 2005 on 263-405 with 32 touchdowns and 7 interceptions and 3,426 yards in 2006 on 289-467 with 37 touchdowns and 7 interceptions)

40) A – Yes (Brady Quinn with 11,476 yards; 900-1,557 with 95 touchdowns and 39 interceptions)

41) C – Jim Seymour (1966 versus Purdue, 276 yards on 13 receptions; Notre Dame 26, Purdue 14)

42) D – Jeff Samardzija (2005; 1,249 yards on 77 receptions and 16.2 yards per reception with 15 touchdowns)

43) C – Jeff Samardzija (2,593 yards on 179 receptions, 14.5 yards per reception with 27 touchdowns)

44) C – 11 (prior to the 8 *AP* titles, Notre Dame won titles in 1924, 1929, and 1930.)

45) B – 3 (Angelo Bertelli 1941, Joe Theismann 1970, Raghib Ismail 1990)

46) C – 2 (Johnny Lujack in 1947 and Leon Hart in 1949)

47) C – 1970 (92.4 offensive plays per game, 924 plays in 10 games)

48) D – 79 (The most of any school. Yale is 2nd with 69 players.)

49) C – 4 (Frank Leahy, 1941, and Ara Parseghian, 1964, were awarded the American Football Coaches Associaton (AFCA) Coach of the Year Award; Ara Parseghain 1964, Lou Holtz 1988, and Charlie Weis 2005 were awarded the Football Writers Association of America (FWAA) Coach of the Year Award)

50) B – Ronald Reagan (This movie elevated Ronald Reagan to 'Star' status from 'B' actor.)

Note: All answers valid as of the end of the 2007 season, unless otherwise indicated in the question itself.

Third Quarter

3-Point Questions

1) How many times has Notre Dame defeated a #1 ranked team?

A) 0
B) 3
C) 6
D) 8

2) What year was the first winning season at Notre Dame (minimum five games)?

A) 1889
B) 1893
C) 1897
D) 1910

3) What year was the first 10 win season at Notre Dame?

A) 1894
B) 1921
C) 1929
D) 1930

4) How much did Army agree to pay Notre Dame, for travel costs, to play a game at West Point in 1913?

A) $100
B) $250
C) $1,000
D) $5,000

5) What year did the Fighting Irish end Georgia Tech's 31-game unbeaten streak?

A) 1953
B) 1957
C) 1988
D) 2002

6) Which Notre Dame quarterback completed the most passes in a bowl game?

A) Joe Montana
B) Brady Quinn
C) Joe Theismann
D) Steve Beurlein

7) Which Notre Dame quarterback has NOT thrown for 2,000 yards or more in a single season?

A) Ron Powlus
B) Joe Montana
C) Daryle Lamonica
D) Rick Mirer

8) What are the most field goals made in a single game by a Notre Dame kicker?

A) 4
B) 5
C) 6
D) 8

9) Which kicker holds the ND record for the longest FG?

A) John Carney
B) Dave Reeve
C) Nicholas Setta
D) Harry Oliver

10) Which former Heisman running back ran for more than 300 yards in a game against the Fighting Irish?

A) Tony Dorsett
B) Eddie George
C) Marcus Allen
D) Reggie Bush

11) Who holds the ND career record for most fumbles recovered?

A) Donald Dykes
B) Steve Lawrence
C) Ross Browner
D) Cedric Figaro

12) Which Fighting Irish free safety shares the NCAA record for most fumble returns for TD in a game?

A) Joe Restic
B) Jeff Burris
C) Glenn Earl
D) Tony Driver

13) What is the Notre Dame record for tackles for loss in one season by a single player?

A) 15
B) 18
C) 28
D) 31

14) Who has the most career interceptions for Notre Dame?

A) Luther Bradley
B) Tom MacDonald
C) Mike Townsend
D) John Lattner

15) Who holds the ND & NCAA career record for most TDs on runbacks (Interceptions, punt & kickoff returns)?

A) Raghib Ismail
B) Tim Brown
C) Allen Rossum
D) Julius Jones

16) How many points were scored against Knute Rockne's Notre Dame Teams in his 122 games as coach?

A) 431
B) 657
C) 957
D) 1,234

17) What trophy does Notre Dame and Michigan State play for?

A) Paul Bunyan Trophy
B) Black Diamond Trophy
C) Heartland Trophy
D) Megaphone Trophy

18) Who holds the Notre Dame record for most punts in a career?

A) Joey Hildbold
B) Blair Kiel
C) Joe Restic
D) Johnny Lattner

19) Paul Hornung never rushed for over 100 yards in a game through his career at Notre Dame?

A) True
B) False

20) What are the most consecutive wins for Notre Dame against USC?

A) 4
B) 7
C) 11
D) 15

21) What are ND's most consecutive losses against USC?

A) 3
B) 5
C) 8
D) 11

22) How many shutouts did Notre Dame record under Coach Knute Rockne?

A) 14
B) 26
C) 28
D) 50

23) How many Notre Dame players are in the College Football Hall of Fame for more than one position?

A) 0
B) 2
C) 5
D) 6

24) Who was the first consensus All-American wide receiver at Notre Dame?

A) Jeff Samardzija
B) Raghib Ismail
C) Tim Brown
D) Pete Demmerle

25) What was Knute Rockne's career winning percentage at Notre Dame?

A) .775
B) .855
C) .881
D) .907

26) Who was ND's first consensus All-American linebacker?

A) Bob Crable
B) Jim Lynch
C) Michael Stonebreaker
D) Bob Golic

27) Who was the first consensus All-American defensive back at Notre Dame?

A) Nick Rassas
B) Tom Schoen
C) Terry Hanratty
D) Todd Lyght

28) The "Blue – Gold" game marks the end of spring practice, what year was the first "Blue – Gold" game?

A) 1947
B) 1953
C) 1959
D) 1968

29) What game did the “Blue – Gold” game replace?

A) “Varsity vs. Old Timers” game
B) Alumni game
C) “Hall of Fame” game
D) “End of Spring” game

30) What was the winning percentage of coaches that lasted one season at Notre Dame?

A) .410
B) .545
C) .691
D) .855

31) Who holds the Notre Dame record for points scored in a season?

A) Art Smith
B) Jerome Bettis
C) Allen Pinkett
D) Autry Denson

32) What year was a Notre Dame team often credited with “inventing” the forward pass?

A) 1897
B) 1905
C) 1913
D) 1922

33) Who was the first black football player at Notre Dame?

A) Wayne Edmonds
B) Dick Washington
C) Tom Gatewood
D) Luther Bradley

34) What is Notre Dame's shared NCAA record for fewest turnovers in a season?

A) 0
B) 5
C) 8
D) 12

35) What are the most consecutive winning seasons that Notre Dame has had?

A) 18
B) 29
C) 36
D) 42

36) What are Notre Dame's most consecutive bowl losses?

A) 2
B) 5
C) 7
D) 9

37) Who was the only three-time captain for Notre Dame?

A) Brady Quinn
B) Jack Mullen
C) Rocky Bleier
D) George Gipp

38) Who was the first black captain for Notre Dame?

A) Tom Gatewood
B) Ross Browner
C) Vagas Ferguson
D) Kory Minor

39) In how many games have Notre Dame opponents been shutout?

A) 189
B) 220
C) 294
D) 331

40) How many times has Notre Dame been shutout?

A) 51
B) 69
C) 87
D) 103

41) What are the most consecutive bowl games Notre Dame has won?

A) 2
B) 3
C) 5
D) 7

42) Who has the ND record for longest run from scrimmage?

A) Rob Livingstone
B) Julius Jones
C) Tony Rice
D) Eric Penick

43) Who has the ND record for longest fumble return?

A) Tom Zbikowski
B) Gerome Sapp
C) Frank Shaughnessy
D) Garron Bible

44) Which of the following Minnesota Viking's "Purple People Eaters" played at Notre Dame?

A) Gary Larsen
B) Jim Marshall
C) Carl Eller
D) Alan Page

45) What is on the sign that all Notre Dame Football players touch for good luck before running out onto the field?

A) "Win One For The Gipper"
B) "Play Like A Champion Today"
C) "We're No. 1"
D) "We Are – Fighting Irish!"

46) What is the mural of Jesus Christ overlooking Notre Dame's stadium referred to?

A) "Coach Jesus"
B) "The Savior At Notre Dame"
C) "Touchdown Jesus"
D) "The Twelfth Player"

47) Who was ND's opponent in the 1992 "Snow Bowl"?

A) Penn State
B) Michigan
C) USC
D) Florida State

48) Which Fighting Irish caught the only TD pass of 1992's Snow Bowl with 20 seconds remaining in the game?

A) Ray Griggs
B) Irv Smith
C) Reggie Brooks
D) Jerome Bettis

49) Who caught QB Rick Mirer's two-point conversion pass to win the 1992 "Snow Bowl"?

A) Reggie Brooks
B) Jerome Bettis
C) Ray Griggs
D) Irv Smith

50) Who was the last Notre Dame running back to rush for more than 200 yards in a game?

A) Reggie Brooks
B) Jerome Bettis
C) Julius Jones
D) Darius Walker

The only football team, professional or college, to have all of its games carried live nationally on radio is – Notre Dame! Since 1968 more than 300 stations in all 50 states have the Fighting Irish on each week of the season. And then there's Television, Notre Dame has appeared on network TV, since 1952, more than any other college, and it's the only school to have all its home games televised nationally.

Third Quarter Answer Key

1) D – 8 (1936, Notre Dame 26, #1 Northwestern 6; 1971, Notre Dame 24, #1 Texas 11; 1973, Notre Dame 24, #1 Alabama 23; 1978, Notre Dame 38, #1 Texas 10; 1982, Notre Dame 31, #1 Pittsburgh 16; 1988, Notre Dame 31, #1 Miami 30; 1990 Notre Dame 21, #1 Colorado 6; 1993, Notre Dame 31, #1 Florida State 24)
2) B – 1893 (4-1-0)
3) B – 1921 (10-1-0)
4) C – $1,000 (Notre Dame 35, Army 13; paid all that money and lost.)
5) A – 1953 (Notre Dame 27, Georgia Tech 14; this was Georgia Tech's 2nd longest winning streak in school history.)
6) B – Brady Quinn (2006 Fiesta Bowl, 29 completions against Ohio State; Notre Dame 20, Ohio State 34)
7) C – Daryle Lamonica (The highest total yards in a season was 821 in 1962.)
8) B – 5 (3 times, Nicholas Setta in 2002 & 2003 and Craig Hentrich in 1990)
9) B – Dave Reeve (53-yarder in 1976 versus Pittsburgh; Notre Dame 10, Pittsburgh 31)
10) A – Tony Dorsett (303 yards on 23 attempts in 1975; Notre Dame 20, Pittsburgh 34)

11) C – Ross Browner (12 fumbles recovered; 1973, 1975-1977)

12) D – Tony Driver (2 fumble returns for TDs shared with 2 other players, 24-yard and 22-yard returns; 2000, Notre Dame 45, Navy 14)

13) C – 28 (Ross Browner in 1976 for a total of 203 yards)

14) A – Luther Bradley (17 interceptions for a total of 218 yards, 1973 and 1975-77)

15) C – Allen Rossum (1994-97; 3 interceptions, 3 punt returns, & 3 kickoff returns)

16) B – 657 (That's 5.4 points given up per game.)

17) D – Megaphone Trophy (Started in 1949 by the Detroit alumni clubs of both schools, Notre Dame has been awarded the Megaphone Trophy 30 times and Michigan State has won it 23 times.)

18) B – Blair Kiel (259 punts from 1980-83; Blair was also a starting QB.)

19) B – False (Paul had 101 yards rushing in 1956 versus Southern Methodist; Notre Dame 13, SMU 19)

20) C – 11 (Notre Dame won every meeting from 1983 through 1993)

21) B – 5 (twice - Notre Dame lost from 1978 to 1982 and from 2002 to 2006)

22) D – 50 (in 122 games, 2nd is Ara Parseghian with 28 shutouts in 116 games)

23) B – 2 (Jerry Groom for center & linebacker and Jim Martin for end & tackle)
24) D – Pete Demmerle (1974, Demmerle had 43 receptions for 667 yards and 6 touchdowns)
25) C – .881 (105-12-5; the best winning percentage of all time for Division 1-A coaches)
26) B – Jim Lynch (In 1966 Lynch had 106 tackles, 2 pass breakups, 3 interceptions, and 1 fumble recovery.)
27) A – Nick Rassas (In 1965 Rassas had 53 tackles, 3 pass breakups, and 6 interceptions with 1 TD as a walk-on.)
28) D – 1968 (Ara Parseghian made the game a game-condition scrimmage between the offense & defense.)
29) A – "Varsity vs. Old Timers" game (The game started in 1929 as a game between current and former Notre Dame players. The varsity won 29 of 36 games.)
30) C – .691 (one-year coaches finished 38-15-2)
31) B – Jerome Bettis (1991; 120 points from 20 touchdowns)
32) C – 1913 (Notre Dame did not invent the forward pass. It was a legal play for many seasons prior to QB Gus Dorais and End Knute Rockne using it to defeat a heavily favored Army team in 1913 - a game that made the forward pass popular.)

33) A and B – Wayne Edmonds (Tackle, 1953-55) and Dick Washington (Halfback, 1953)

34) C – 8 (2000 season; 4 fumbles lost and 4 interceptions lost; tied with Clemson of 1940 and Miami (Ohio) of 1966)

35) D – 42 (1889 to 1932 (no teams in 1890 and 1891); this is an NCAA all-time record.)

36) D – 9 (Currently the longest streak in FBS)

37) B – Jack Mullen (captain in 1897, '98, and '99, played 6 seasons from 1894 to 1899)

38) A – Tom Gatewood (Co-captain 1971, his career reception total of 157 was the Notre Dame record until broken in 2006.)

39) C – 294 shutouts (That is 26% of the 1,132 games played.)

40) B – 69 (only 6% of the 1,132 games played.)

41) C – 5 (1973 Sugar Bowl, 1974 Orange Bowl, 1976 Gator Bowl, 1977 and 1978 Cotton Bowl)

42) A – Rob Livingstone (92 yards against USC in 1947; Notre Dame 38, USC 7)

43) C – Frank Shaughnessy (107 yards; the field measured 110 yards in 1904 with TDs worth 5 points; Notre Dame 5, Kansas 24)

44) D – Alan Page (DE, 1964-1966; played 15 seasons in the NFL, received his Law Degree in 1978, and now serves on the Minnesota Supreme Court)

45) B – "Play Like A Champion Today" (Arguably one of the great traditions at Notre Dame, started under Ara Parseghian in the early 1960s.)

46) C – "Touchdown Jesus" (A 132'-tall stone mosaic on the south wall of the Hesburgh Library depicts Jesus Christ with his arms upraised like that of an official signaling a touchdown.)

47) A – Penn State (#8 Notre Dame 17, #22 Penn State 16)

48) B – Jerome Bettis (4-yard touchdown pass)

49) A – Reggie Brooks (Rick Mirer scrambled to the right and found Reggie Brooks in the back of the end zone for the win.)

50) C – Julius Jones (218 yards on 23 attempts, November 29, 2003; Notre Dame 57, Stanford 7)

Note: All answers valid as of the end of the 2007 season, unless otherwise indicated in the question itself.

1) Which team has Notre Dame NEVER beaten?

A) Florida State
B) Miami (Ohio)
C) Georgia
D) Kansas

2) Which Notre Dame head coach recorded only one shutout over an opponent in his career?

A) Tyrone Willingham
B) Bob Davie
C) Gerry Faust
D) Hugh Devore

3) How many teams does Notre Dame have at least 50 wins against?

A) 1
B) 2
C) 4
D) 6

4) The Notre Dame record for consecutive seasons with a 1,000-yard passer is 12 years?

A) True
B) False

5) What number did Notre Dame Heisman Trophy winner Tim Brown wear?

A) 80
B) 81
C) 83
D) 87

6) Who holds the Notre Dame rushing record for highest average yards per carry?

A) Jerome Bettis
B) Autry Denson
C) Don Miller
D) George Gipp

7) Excluding Purdue, who is the last school from Indiana to beat the Fighting Irish?

A) Wabash
B) Valparaiso
C) DePauw
D) Indiana

8) What year did ND play its entire season on the road?

A) 1903
B) 1914
C) 1929
D) 1943

9) How many former Notre dame players are in the College Football Hall of Fame?

A) 26
B) 31
C) 35
D) 41

10) When was the last time Notre Dame was shutout?

A) 1978
B) 1987
C) 1998
D) 2003

11) How many QB four-year starters has Notre Dame had?

A) 1
B) 3
C) 5
D) 6

12) What are the fewest points Notre Dame has scored at home for an entire season?

A) 0
B) 10
C) 13
D) 17

13) What is the Notre Dame record for consecutive wins?

A) 17
B) 23
C) 42
D) 56

14) What is the Notre Dame record for consecutive games without a defeat (wins and ties)?

A) 25
B) 29
C) 39
D) 47

15) Which team has Notre Dame beaten the most to open the season?

A) Northwestern
B) Pittsburgh
C) Kalamazoo
D) Purdue

16) What year did Notre Dame play in front of over 1 million fans at home and away games?

A) 1999
B) 2002
C) 2005
D) 2006

Fourth Quarter

4-Point Questions

17) What was the largest single crowd to watch a Notre Dame Football game?

A) 80,795
B) 93,778
C) 106,508
D) 120,000

18) What are the most points scored in a quarter by the Fighting Irish?

A) 32
B) 35
C) 40
D) 56

19) Who led the nation in rushing yards in 1943?

A) Creighton Miller
B) Julie Rykovich
C) Jim Mello
D) Bob Livingstone

20) Who holds the NCAA record for most consecutive field goals made from 40 to 49 yards?

A) Garrett Rivas
B) John Carney
C) Nick Setta
D) Mike Johnston

Fourth Quarter *4-Point Questions*

21) Which game of the year has ND won the most times?

A) 1st game
B) 2nd game
C) 7th game
D) 8th game

22) Which game of the year has ND lost the most times?

A) 1st game
B) 3rd game
C) 10th game
D) 12th game

23) Who was the first Notre Dame coach to win 10 games in his first season?

A) Ara Parseghian
B) Charlie Weis
C) Lou Holtz
D) Tyrone Willingham

24) Which team has Notre Dame NEVER played?

A) Yale
B) Rutgers
C) Louisville
D) Cincinnati

25) Notre Dame's QB Tom Clements was also recruited by which school to play basketball?

A) North Carolina
B) UCLA
C) Houston
D) St. Johns

26) What did coaches Rockne, Leahy, Parseghain, Devine, and Holtz do in each of their 3rd seasons?

A) Had a losing record
B) Went undefeated
C) Won a National Championship
D) Took a leave of absence

27) Who is the only Heisman Trophy winner to play on a Notre Dame team with a losing record?

A) John Huarte
B) Leon Hart
C) Paul Hornung
D) Angelo Bertelli

28) What decade did ND have the best winning percentage?

A) 1900s
B) 1920s
C) 1940s
D) 1970s

Fourth Quarter

4-Point Questions

29) What decade did ND have the worst winning percentage?

A) 1880s
B) 1930s
C) 1960s
D) 2000s

30) How many decades has Notre Dame won at least 80% of their games?

A) 1
B) 2
C) 3
D) 4

31) How many overtime-games has the Fighting Irish won?

A) 0
B) 2
C) 3
D) 5

32) Which special teams player blocked a field goal attempt against Air Force, in 2000, to send the game into OT?

A) Mark Mitchell
B) Donald Dykes
C) Glenn Earl
D) Grant Irons

33) How many games has Notre Dame won as time expired?

A) 0
B) 2
C) 5
D) 7

34) How many games has Notre Dame lost as time expired?

A) 0
B) 1
C) 3
D) 6

35) What defense did Notre Dame use to defeat the undefeated Texas Longhorns in the 1971 Cotton Bowl?

A) Mirror defense
B) 7-diamond
C) Nickel
D) 33 stack

36) How many times has Notre Dame appeared in the Cotton/Orange/Sugar/Fiesta/Rose bowls combined?

A) 15
B) 19
C) 21
D) 28

Fourth Quarter *4-Point Questions*

37) What was the best winning percentage of a Notre Dame Head coach that lasted only one season?

A) .500
B) .675
C) .755
D) .889

38) Which former two-way starter won a shot-put Gold Medal at the 1938 Lithuanian Olympics?

A) Ed Beinor
B) Joe Kuharich
C) Joe Zwers
D) John Yonakor

39) What was the best winning percentage of a Notre Dame Head coach that lasted two seasons?

A) .500
B) .750
C) .933
D) 1.000

40) How many Fighting Irish have won the Lombardi Award?

A) 1
B) 2
C) 4
D) 5

41) How many Fighting Irish have won the Outland Trophy?

A) 0
B) 1
C) 3
D) 5

42) How many Fighting Irish have won the Butkus Award?

A) 0
B) 1
C) 2
D) 4

43) How many Notre Dame players were suspended in 1974 due to a controversial dorm violation?

A) 1
B) 3
C) 4
D) 6

44) How many former Notre Dame players have been enshrined into the NFL Football Hall of Fame?

A) 4
B) 9
C) 12
D) 14

45) How many first round NFL Draft picks has ND produced?

A) 29
B) 41
C) 44
D) 59

46) Has a Notre Dame player ever won the Bronko Nagurski Award?

A) Yes
B) No

47) Who was captain and defensive tackle leader of Notre Dame's 1966 National Championship team?

A) Jim Carroll
B) Jim Lynch
C) Alan Page
D) Pete Duranko

48) What college did Frank Leahy coach before becoming the head coach at Notre Dame?

A) Missouri
B) Miami (OH)
C) Boston College
D) Fordham

49) What team did Notre Dame play in Tokyo, Japan in 1979?

A) Army
B) Miami (Fla.)
C) UCLA
D) San Diego State

50) Notre Dame and Maryland played in the last Kickoff Classic in 2002 with the Fighting Irish winning 22 – 0, who was named the most valuable player?

A) Nicholas Setta
B) Shane Walton
C) Carlyle Holiday
D) Vontez Duff

Fourth Quarter Fighting Irish Cool Fact

"Win One for the Gipper" was a request from Notre Dame legend George Gipp to Coach Knute Rockne from his deathbed in 1920. It later turned into one of the most inspirational pep talks ever. In November of 1928, Notre Dame found itself a big underdog to an undefeated Army team in Yankee Stadium. Army didn't have a chance after Coach Rockne delivered George Gipp's inspirational request, the Irish won 12 – 6! As Jack Chevigny scores the first of two Notre Dame touchdowns he shouts "That one was for the Gipper!"

Fourth Quarter Answer Key

1) C – Georgia (played one time in 1980; Georgia was led by RB Herschel Walker. Notre Dame 10, Georgia 17)
2) B – Bob Davie (1998; Notre Dame 30, Navy 0; coached 5 years from 1997 to 2001)
3) B – 2 (Navy 70 and Purdue 51)
4) A – True (from 1988-99; Tony Rice with 1,176 yards in 1988, 1,122 yards in 1989, Rick Mirer with 1,824 yards in 1990, 2,117 yards in 1991, 1,876 yards in 1992, Kevin McDougal with 1,541 yards in 1993, Ron Powlus with 1,729 yards in 1994, 1,853 yards in 1995, 1,942 yards in 1996, 2,078 yards in 1997, and Jarious Jackson with 1,740 yards in 1998, 2,753 yards in 1999)
5) B – 81
6) C – Don Miller (6.8 average yards per carry on 1,933 yards in 283 carries from 1922-24)
7) D – Indiana (1950 Notre Dame 7, Indiana 20)
8) C – 1929 (Excavation was under way on the new stadium; Notre Dame went 9-0-0 and won a National Championship.)
9) D – 41 (This is more than any other school.)
10) D – 2003 (At home, Notre Dame 0, Florida State 37)

11) C – 5 (Gus Dorias 1910-13, Blair Kiel 1980-83, Steve Beuerlein 1983-86, Ron Powlus 1994-97, and Brady Quinn 2003-06)

12) A – 0 (1933; Notre Dame played four home games and was shutout in all of them.)

13) B – 23 (From September 10, 1988 until November 25, 1989; all under Coach Lou Holtz)

14) C – 39 (37 wins and 2 ties, from September 28, 1946 until October 30, 1950; under Coach Frank Leahy)

15) A – Northwestern (played 10 season-openers with a 9-1 record)

16) B – 2002 (1,008,693 fans in 13 games, an average of 77,592 per game)

17) D – 120,000 (at Soldiers Field in Chicago, twice; 1927 Notre Dame 7, USC 6 and 1928, Notre Dame 7, Navy 0)

18) C – 40 (Notre Dame scored 40 points in the second quarter against Pittsburgh in 1996. Notre Dame 60, Pittsburgh 6)

19) A – Creighton Miller (911 yards, son of Red Miller who was a great running back in 1906-09, and nephew of Don Miller who also was a great running back in 1922-24)

20) B – John Carney (12 consecutive in the 1984 and 1985 seasons; 10 for 10 in 1984)

21) A – 1st game (Notre Dame is 96-14-5 in the 1st game of the season.)
22) B – 3rd game (Notre Dame is 83-31-1 in the 3rd game of the season.)
23) D – Tyrone Willingham (2002, 10-3-0)
24) C – Louisville
25) A – North Carolina (Dean Smith wanted him to be the Tar Heel's point guard.)
26) C – Won a National Championship (Rockne in 1920, Leahy in 1943, Parseghian in 1966, Devine in 1977, and Holtz in 1988)
27) C – Paul Hornung (Notre Dame's record was 2-8 in 1956 when Paul Hornung won the Heisman; he led the Irish in passing and rushing. He also returned kick-offs and punts and made 55 tackles with 2 interceptions on defense.)
28) C – 1940s (82-9-6, .876)
29) D – 2000s (Through 2007 the Irish are 54-31 [.635].)
30) D – 4 (1910s 63-7-6 [.868]; 1920s 83-11-3 [.871], 1940s 82-9-6 [.876], and 1970s 91-22-0 [.803])
31) B – 2 (Notre Dame has been in only 6 OT games, winning in 2000 Notre Dame 34, Air Force 31 and in 2003 Notre Dame 29, Washington State 26)
32) C – Glenn Earl (a freshman back-up at Strong Safety)

33) D – 7 (1961, Notre Dame 17, Syracuse 15; 1979, (Cotton Bowl) Notre Dame 35, Houston 34; 1980, Notre Dame 29, Michigan 27; 1986, Notre Dame 38, USC 37; 1996, Notre Dame 27, Texas 24; 2000, Notre Dame 23, Purdue 21; 2003, Notre Dame 27, Navy 24)

34) C – 3 (1982; Notre Dame 13, Arizona 16; 1993, Notre Dame 39, Boston College 41; 1999, Notre Dame 37, Stanford 40)

35) A – Mirror defense (Ara Parseghian had each of his linebackers mirror a Longhorn back. This was very effective against the wishbone offense. Notre Dame 24, Texas 11)

36) C – 21 (7 Cotton Bowls, 5 Orange Bowls, 4 Sugar Bowls, 4 Fiesta Bowls, and 1 Rose Bowl)

37) D – .889 (Victor M. Place, 1908, 8-1)

38) A – Ed Beinor (Nicknamed “Beefy”, he tossed the shot-put 47 feet 11 inches.)

39) C – .933 (John L. Marks, 1911-12, 13-0-2)

40) C – 4 (1971, DE, Walt Patulski; 1977, DE, Ross Browner; 1990, DT, Chris Zorich; and 1993, Aaron Taylor)

41) C – 3 (1946, OT, George Connor; 1948, OG, Bill Fischer; and 1976, DE, Ross Browner)

42) A – 0 (Michael Stonebreaker was a finalist in 1988 & 1990 and Courtney Watson was a finalist in 2002)

43) D – 6 (Ross Browner, Luther Bradley, Al Hunter, Willie Fry, Roy Henry, and Dan Knott; females were present in their rooms past curfew)

44) B – 9 (1963 Curly Lambeau, 1964 George Trafton, 1968 Wayne Milner, 1975 George Connor, 1986 Paul Hornung, 1988 Alan Page, 2000 Joe Montana, 2001 Nick Buoniconti, & 2002 Dave Casper)

45) D – 59 (ranks 3rd all-time; USC is 1st with 67 and Ohio State is 2nd with 65)

46) B – No (CB Shane Walton in 2002 was the first and only finalist for the award; T, Bronko Nagurski, Jr. played for Notre Dame 1956 and 1957)

47) B – Jim Lynch (LB, 1964-66, had 106 tackles in 1966; drafted by Kansas City in the 2nd round and helped them win the Super Bowl in 1968)

48) C – Boston College (1939-40, 20-2 record)

49) B – Miami (Fla.) (A regular season game called the Mirage Bowl, Notre Dame 40, Miami (Fla.) 15; 62,000 fans, Tokyo Olympic Memorial Stadium)

50) A – Nicholas Setta (kicked 5 field goals)

Note: All answers valid as of the end of the 2007 season, unless otherwise indicated in the question itself.

Overtime Bonus *4-Point Questions*

1) How many times has Notre Dame led the nation in scoring defense?

A) 0
B) 1
C) 3
D) 6

2) How many times has ND led the nation in total offense?

A) 1
B) 3
C) 5
D) 7

3) How did the great Notre Dame Coach Knute Rockne die?

A) Train crash
B) Car crash
C) Plane crash
D) Natural causes

4) For what notable precedent is Knute Rockne's funeral known?

A) Televised live nationally
B) Broadcast live nationally on radio
C) First non-president to lie in state at the Capitol
D) Attended by the Pope

5) In the movie "Rudy", in what role did Daniel "Rudy" Ruettiger make a cameo appearance?

A) The waterboy
B) A grounds keeper
C) A fan in the stands
D) A steel mill worker

6) What was the nickname of the starting offensive line that played with the "Four Horsemen"?

A) Seven Mules
B) 7 Blocks of Granite
C) The Desperados
D) Monsters of the Midway

7) What year did a ND QB lead the nation in pass efficiency?

A) 1949
B) 1967
C) 2005
D) 2006

8) Who kicked the winning FG in the season-opener against Michigan in 1988's National Championship Season?

A) John Carney
B) Craig Hentrich
C) Nicholas Setta
D) Reggie Ho

9) Which former Notre Dame player was 1948's "Mr. Irrelevant", a name given to the last player selected in the NFL Draft of each year?

A) John Panelli
B) Art Statuto
C) Bill Fischer
D) George Ratterman

10) What year did players from Notre Dame become four of the top ten selections in the NFL Draft?

A) 1946
B) 1954
C) 1988
D) 1993

Overtime Bonus Answer Key

1) B – 1 (1946 giving up only 2.7 points per game)
2) B – 3 (1943 with 418 avg. yards per game, 1946 with 441.3 avg. yards per game, 1949 with 434.8 avg. yards per game)
3) C – Plane crash (March 31, 1931 on a flight from Kansas City to Los Angeles, Transcontinental-Western flight 599 went down due to icing in a field near Bazaar, Kansas.)
4) B – Broadcast live nationally on radio (also broadcasted live to Europe, South America, and Asia, on CBS Radio)
5) C – A fan in the stands (There's a brief close-up of him in the stands watching himself play the final play of the Georgia Tech game.)
6) A – Seven Mules (C, Adam Walsh and T, Edgar Miller along with each of the Four Horsemen are in the National Football Hall of Fame, that makes 6 members of the 1924 Notre Dame team elected to the Hall of Fame.)
7) A – 1949 (Bob Williams, a rating of 159.1)
8) D – Reggie Ho (a 27-yarder with 1:13 remaining; a walk-on and former soccer player from St. Louis High School in Honolulu, Hawaii)

9) C – Bill Fischer (taken with the 7th pick of the 32nd round, 300th overall, by the Chicago Cardinals; Bill stayed in school, won the Outland Trophy in 1948 and became the 10th pick in the 1st round of 1949 by the same Chicago Cardinals)

10) A – 1946 (QB Frank Dancewicz No.1 by the Boston Yanks, QB Johnny Lujack No. 4 by the Chicago Bears, T George Connor No. 5 by the New York Giants, and Emil "Red" Sitko No. 10 by the Los Angeles Rams)

Note: All answers valid as of the end of the 2007 season, unless otherwise indicated in the question itself.

Player / Team Score Sheet

Fighting Irishology Trivia Challenge

Name:______________________________

First Quarter				Second Quarter				Third Quarter				Fourth Quarter				Overtime	
1		26		1		26		1		26		1		26		1	
2		27		2		27		2		27		2		27		2	
3		28		3		28		3		28		3		28		3	
4		29		4		29		4		29		4		29		4	
5		30		5		30		5		30		5		30		5	
6		31		6		31		6		31		6		31		6	
7		32		7		32		7		32		7		32		7	
8		33		8		33		8		33		8		33		8	
9		34		9		34		9		34		9		34		9	
10		35		10		35		10		35		10		35		10	
11		36		11		36		11		36		11		36			
12		37		12		37		12		37		12		37			
13		38		13		38		13		38		13		38			
14		39		14		39		14		39		14		39			
15		40		15		40		15		40		15		40			
16		41		16		41		16		41		16		41			
17		42		17		42		17		42		17		42			
18		43		18		43		18		43		18		43			
19		44		19		44		19		44		19		44			
20		45		20		45		20		45		20		45			
21		46		21		46		21		46		21		46			
22		47		22		47		22		47		22		47			
23		48		23		48		23		48		23		48			
24		49		24		49		24		49		24		49			
25		50		25		50		25		50		25		50			
___x 1 =___				___x 2 =___				___x 3 =___				___x 4 =___				___x 4 =___	

Multiply total number correct by point value/quarter to calculate totals for each quarter.

Add total of all quarters below.

Total Points:________

Thank you for playing Fighting Irishology Trivia Challenge.

Additional score sheets are available at:
www.TriviaGameBooks.com

Player / Team Score Sheet

FIGHTING IRISHOLOGY TRIVIA CHALLENGE

Name:____

First Quarter				Second Quarter				Third Quarter				Fourth Quarter				Overtime	
1		26		1		26		1		26		1		26		1	
2		27		2		27		2		27		2		27		2	
3		28		3		28		3		28		3		28		3	
4		29		4		29		4		29		4		29		4	
5		30		5		30		5		30		5		30		5	
6		31		6		31		6		31		6		31		6	
7		32		7		32		7		32		7		32		7	
8		33		8		33		8		33		8		33		8	
9		34		9		34		9		34		9		34		9	
10		35		10		35		10		35		10		35		10	
11		36		11		36		11		36		11		36			
12		37		12		37		12		37		12		37			
13		38		13		38		13		38		13		38			
14		39		14		39		14		39		14		39			
15		40		15		40		15		40		15		40			
16		41		16		41		16		41		16		41			
17		42		17		42		17		42		17		42			
18		43		18		43		18		43		18		43			
19		44		19		44		19		44		19		44			
20		45		20		45		20		45		20		45			
21		46		21		46		21		46		21		46			
22		47		22		47		22		47		22		47			
23		48		23		48		23		48		23		48			
24		49		24		49		24		49		24		49			
25		50		25		50		25		50		25		50			
___x 1 =____				___x 2 =____				___x 3 =____				___x 4 =____				___x 4 =____	

Multiply total number correct by point value/quarter to calculate totals for each quarter.

Add total of all quarters below.

Total Points:________

Thank you for playing Fighting Irishology Trivia Challenge.

Additional score sheets are available at:
www.TriviaGameBooks.com